PAWS & ALL
TALES AND TIPS

PAWS & ALL
TALES AND TIPS

A Comedic Guide to At-Home Dog Grooming

EVELYN GONDER

LIV
ONE CO.

Liv, Learn, Create ™

livonecompany.com

Library of Congress Control Number: 2024922518

All rights reserved.

ISBNs

979-8-9861874-6-4 (print), 979-8-9861874-7-1 (ebook)

Printed in the United States of America

I am thankful to God for not just one thing but for all things: my beloved ancestors – grandfather, grandmother, mother, sister, and nephews – now resting on the wings of heaven. To my loving family and friends, who constantly inspire me to keep going and reach for my dreams, and to my loyal pitbull, Freeway, who stands by me through it all – I love you. I'm so incredibly proud of myself for persevering and accomplishing my first literary work, rooted in my passion for caring for dogs. Truly blessed to be a part of your lives.

With love,

Evelyn

CONTENTS

CHAPTER 1

Saga of the Shih Tzu -Ah,The Majestic Shih Tzu

Shih Tzus, Shih Tzus, Shih Tzus. Oh... Shih Tzus, you notorious snorer, you! The glamour of it all! We simply adore these fur babies because these "Happiness Hackers" sure know how to sprinkle joy with their lovable, bubblicious, contagious personalities.

They're a pet owner's dream come true. But let's cut the cutey patootie and get real. Just like a grumpy old grandpa who's set in his ways, Shih Tzus can develop a bit of stubbornness as they age, especially when it comes to grooming. Well, isn't this just a bag of sunshine and rainbows? That old pooch!

Aht! Aht! Not so fast. Maybe they're not quite as old as those long-flowing hairs might suggest. After all, hints of resistance can start early for these little Dukes and Duchesses, as early as 12 weeks, because, let's face it, they're not always the biggest fans of grooming... until they get used to it. Well—actually... some of them never quite get used to it.

Although Shih Tzus are great house dogs, with their charm and affectionate nature, coaxing them into the grooming routine can sometimes feel like organizing a zoo. Quite chaotic. Right?

While herding cats at a dog show might seem easier than grooming a Shih Tzu, it's most common to keep their coats short year-round because Shih Tzus can easily tangle. That's why it's crucial to maintain a weekly brushing routine, preferably with a slicker brush.

Once you've armed yourself with all your grooming gear, it's time to tackle that buzz cut with clippers to ensure an even trim all around. And when it comes to styling their legs and feet, be prepared to employ some fancy footwork — think of it as boxing, dodging those tiny strike bites they're prone to when handling those sensitive areas.

Why, you ask? It's all because of their regal arrogance. To Shih Tzus, humans are merely subjects to be tolerated, and certain parts of their bodies are off-limits.

With shears and thinners as sharp as Excalibur, trimming isn't just about blunt cuts; it's about catching those pesky fly-aways, too.

"Yap, yap, yap!" There it is, that high-pitched, short, and sharp barking, echoing through the air as you wield those buzzing clippers through their silky-soft, floor-length locks. Oh yes, they've certainly got your attention now, so steady those hands and keep your focus as you work your magic.

Now that all that snipping and clipping hullabaloo is behind us, let's saunter back over to attend to that little tyke's head, shall we? But tread lightly, for we must preserve that precious, wubbly dubbly face of theirs.

With a fine-tooth comb, gently tease the hair away from those twinkling eyes and delicate ears. Secure it into a pony with a snag-free elastic band, being careful not to pull too tightly and cause any discomfort. Don't bulge the eyes any more than the dice between their itty-bitty noses.

Depending on how much your heir prances about the palace, you may need to employ a "Buzz Beast" or "Zap Zapper," code name for the Nail Dremel or nail trimmer, to tidy up those nails. Why the code names, you ask? Well, we wouldn't want to spook them. Just the mention of a "drill," and they're back to their "yap, yap, yap!" antics. And don't forget to wield the clippers to tidy up any unruly foot fur.

With a few more dainty finishing touches — a top knot here, a regal garment like bows, bowties, or a bandanna there, and perhaps a spritz of a bold fragrance — they're ready to be released from the chambers of torture and set free to roam the palace once more.

What a relief! They've made it through unscathed. So, scratch that — no need to send them all the way back to their origins in Tibet. They can remain your loyal little royal pup, safe and sound. Take a deep breath, count to three, and let out a resounding "Woosah!"

Stop the presses! I mean it, grab your phone, hold it up high, and tap that camera button because there's just one more thing. Now that your little rascal is back to their frolicking ways, they're primed and ready for their social media debut.

Click, click, click — snap away because your fur baby is Instagram, Facebook, and TikTok gold! It's high time to unleash their undeniable cuteness and showcase their fresh new look to the world.

Can you believe they even tried to dodge the camera after that epic grooming session? Their charm is downright irresistible and simply must be shared far and wide. They're practically magnets for engagement!

Shih Tzus have a knack for stirring up

overwhelming emotional responses from online audiences, racking up views, likes, and shares faster than a cheetah. So why not jump on that bandwagon? The Shih Tzu online fanbase is eagerly awaiting their arrival.

Time to break out the hashtags! #ShihTzus, #ShihTzuLovers, #ShihTzuNation. Let's get those likes pouring in because you and your cuddle buddy might as well start trending.

All that hard work for nothing? Not a chance!

CHAPTER 2

Pitty Powerful Pitbull

Ladies and gentlemen, gather round, gather round! Well, maybe not that close as we attempt to groom this big-hearted, life-sized, fire-breathing, muscular dinosaur. Otherwise known as the Pitbull.

Now, brace yourselves and give that attractive pitty a big ol' charming smile because we are about to dive into caring for one of a doggy's greatest self-defenses and more. They might not likey, but it's got to be done.

We will start by attempting to trim its talons...oops, I mean toenails. Tah hee hee. Yes, we need to take care of its clutchy claws. Legend has it that Pitbulls are almost never cooperative when getting a manicure. Can you believe it? One could even be mauled to death! Oh my, clutches pearls.

Simmer, simmer. That was indeed a bit dramatic, but by following this initial step first, you'll be in a much safer position to complete this grooming process. Can we say, "Safe haven me, please?"

"Trust it like a dog with bacon" — an oxymoron incoming! Helpful, healthy treats, kind words, and loads of encouragement, much like a true pup owner's reassuring hug, assist in the process. "Soothe them," they say, and it can often do the trick! Easy enough, right?

Now, by this time, you should be ready for step two. Scurry, scurry! Yes, scurry, your loyal Highness, to the doggy pool or luxurious retreat to bathe the baby dino.

Hold it! Who goes there! Spraying water directly on your miniature T-Rex is a big no-no. Don't do it! Or it may not end well for you.

For once, be a smarty-pants and hold the sprayer or stream the water closely to the canine's body. This step three method provides a tolerable level of comfort for them. Keeping their sensitive skin in mind, use a reputable shampoo and conditioner designed for their breed and personal needs.

And don't forget to gently rub a dub-dub them in that tub. Hey, a rubber duckie toy may just top off their grooming experience!

One last thing, unless your handsome pitty is shivering away due to cold temperatures, using a dryer isn't necessary.

Finally, time to throw in the towel. Ladies and gentlemen, with that being said, this wraps up our itty-bitty dino grooming exhibit.

CHAPTER 3

Yay Yorkshire Terrier

Well, well, well, we've arrived at the "yay high" doggie woggiez that are all bark AND bite! Ooouuuccchhh! There is a lot to be said about these poochie woochiez, better known as Yorkshire Terriers or Yorkies for short. They are cute, dainty, feisty, and brave.

What's even more fascinating is that these toy dogs are known for being some of the smallest dogs in the world. Winner, winner! Hand them their championship belt for this distinguished title! Never mind, that's probably too heavy for their miniature bodies.

Give them a mini ribbon instead because that's one heck of a dog title to hold! No wonder every "It" girl and rich guy wants one. They are portable and adorable and quite the accessory to the chic style of their owner.

Now, time to get to the nitty gritty grooming adventures and techniques for caring for these loveable creatures. Yowch! That little nibbler just bit me. Ahh, it didn't hurt though. Yorkie-pooh is just being curious and playful as we prepare to give it some TLC! Oh, that's just tender, loving care.

When grooming these tenacious yet affectionate terriers, prepare to encounter one of their most irritating and vexing traits — their yelping!

"Yip, yip, yip!" YUP! That's it right there. That's the sound. Do not be mistaken, the chord of their high-pitched barking is usually on constant replay.

Cry me a river — and not the beautiful way an opera singer brings the crowd to tears. Not even a good pair of earphones will help — well, maybe! Good luck! Chop, chop, go get them — now. Make it quick!

Now that things appear to be a tad bit quieter, we'll focus on the Yorkie's fur. Most Yorkies have a single coat of hair. Choosing what haircare tool works best for them, between pin brushes or slick brushes, trimmers, and even combs, is the better route.

Though you can use many tools to groom them, these dogs have a funny way of letting you know what feels best to them. "Yip, yip, yip!" See, told yah!

Next, there are three different directions to follow when performing maintenance on these pups. The classic puppy cut requires brushing and cutting due to their wavy hair, while the canine cut consists of the shave-down method for a nice, smooth finish.

Last but not least, Yorkies with the "drop coat" have fine, straight, textured hair that requires combing and brushing only to maintain their silky, flowy look.

It's also good to know that Yorkie's hair types make them great for people who experience allergies. They have minimal shedding compared to other popular dog breeds.

Wow! Look at that. You've got it. You're on your way to mastering taming your Yorkie's coat.

Following, Yorkie's nail care is just as important. Surprisingly, these tiny dogs can grow very long nails. How dangerous! Their nails are mostly black in color and quite noticeable when left unclipped.

Trimming them is another task in itself. They can get the wiggling, moving, and grooving. Therefore, a helping hand may sometimes do the trick in keeping them still to attend to their claws and cuticles.

To wrap up this Yorkshire Terrier grooming adventure and technique, it's good to know that giving them a warm bath every four to six weeks is necessary to maintain good health. Yorkies hate being cold, so drying them with a warm towel will soothe their soul. Tah dah!

Here's the fun part. Your Yorkie is ready to be dressed. Give them a sense of style by putting them in stylish clothes like dresses, shirts, collars, bows, and bowties with pops of color.

Don't forget their bells and whistles for

outrageous compliments from onlookers wherever you and your pup go. After all, all that hard work wasn't for nothing.

CHAPTER 4

Got Darn Goldendoodle

Opening scene. Brush, brush, brush, and after that, brush, brush, and brush some more for good measure. In Scene One, the Goldendoodle will react as if it is being scalped by a thick, slick brush — like it's a straight razor. No need to fret. There's no tearing happening over here.

Standing ovation for this lapdog's great acting skills. How performative, should we say?

Well, unless they're matted. In that case, they are acting accordingly — and what a meltdown that can be.

This first scene can be quite entertaining. Brushing its curly coats daily might just be the most critical part of this movie. Don't fast-forward this scene! If it's skipped over, the ending of this motion picture will result in a complete shave-down.

Trust and believe, you'll be dodging tomatoes from movie critics who will inform audiences it's a film not worth seeing. Eek!

They're kind of right, though. A strange four-legged drunk-looking doggy wandering your home during the night as if they belonged on the streets is not it.

Avoid poor ratings; gently caress those woolly waves and watch your friendly paw pal show off its best acting skills, displaying their adorable, bubbly, loving personality.

In Scene Two, it's time to pluck away! Plick, plick, plick, tweeze, tweeze, tweeze, and tug, tug, tug — but do it gingerly! Your movie lead, your Darn Doodle-baby, has sensitive skin, so handle it with care as you pluck those hairs out of its ears.

Tisk, tisk, no roughness allowed!

Clean their ear canals delicately, removing those pesky stray hairs. Keep those listening tunnels squeaky clean to ward off infection and ensure your bouncy protagonist stays fresh and sweet-smelling.

Eww, no one likes a stinky star!

Next up — the plot thickens! Just kidding. The only thing thickening is the luxurious lather of shampoo and conditioner. Mmm, what's the scent? A blissful blend of tropical aromas, like papaya and coconut, fills the air.

After a thorough rinse, your canine cutie will be irresistibly squeezable. And who knows, this delightful bathing scene might just warrant a sequel in this never-ending story of grooming adventures!

Alrighty now, this doggy film is picking up. We've arrived at the longest and most drawn-out scene, but let the tape roll. It's time for... dun, dun, duuun, DRYING! Aah! The moviegoers shriek in fear.

Simmer, simmer. It's only a high-velocity dryer. This powerful tool will help make drying time a little faster.

Wallah! Main character energy is fully activated. The headliner, *Darn Doodle*, for short, will offer you plenty of paws to manicure and groom. No yawning — there's still an hour to go in on this flick, and your Goldendoodle is here for the theatrics. Rest assured, there will be a few double-takes and bathroom breaks.

Use your preferred clip comb on your pup to handle hairs and tangles, along with a steel comb to create the perfect silhouette. Curved shears always come in handy; these cutters will direct the rounding of their head and feet for that pom-pom effect.

Awe, how cute. Now, trim their nails meticulously and feather their plume tail.

"It's a wrap!" yells the director — that's you — and your charming Goldendoodle, the star.

Your grooming creativity is simply a masterpiece. Siskel and Ebert give *Darn Golden Doodle* two thumbs up! A box office hit!

CHAPTER 5

Quest Into the Nova Scotia Duck Trolling Retriever

Prepare to embark on a delightful journey as you fully groom the rare, charming Nova Scotia Duck Trolling Retriever — a rare find breed. This ride is an emotional rollercoaster — so buckle up and hold on tight. Wheeee!

Love is definitely in the air with these affectionate retriever pups. Can't you feel it?

With their sweet demeanor and droopy almond-shaped eyes, they'll make you feel GUILTY, as if you're about to commit a serious crime.

But don't worry; your intelligent pup will soon realize you're just giving them some much-needed care to enhance their appearance and ensure their hygiene. It's going to be doooogggg good! Oops, I mean, all good!

Whine, whine, and more whine — and not the kind you sip! Ha! Ha! Yep, that's the sound of your squeaky pooh-bear with their shivering bark and squeal. Arf! Arf! To them, water is like a streaming creek flowing into a river. Can we say... bathtime!

Feeling a bit CONFUSED? Ha-ha! You should be. These peculiar, funny furry friends have fluffy feathers and beautiful, shiny, subtle cherry coats that are water-resistant. Well, yah don't say! Geez!

Drenching them lovingly with water is a must. Because these eager-to-please pups go along with the flow, they'll tolerate the delightful wash. Splish splash! What a fun water dip on this amusing coaster ride.

Hold up, wait a minute! Special alert incoming: bathe your baby with fragrance-free shampoo. This is a must to protect their sensitive skin.

Feeling PRODUCTIVE yet? Well, the quest isn't over. Onward we go! Set your dryer to a cool to medium-low setting, leaving you both with the SATISFYING feeling that you're protecting your little Nova Scotia from heat damage and skin irritation.

No time for trolling around now — it's time to brush your high-spirited little duck-hunting dog's golden-red or dark copper with blended coats. Brush softly to remove any matted hair. This is a pretty easy task for these medium-sized crimson Tollers since their matted hairs are usually limited to behind their ears and under their bellies.

Hands up! We're about to speed down this coaster's steepest drop. Woohoo! Grab the thinning shears to define their front legs and haunches. This is easy work because these simple breeds are a breeze to trim.

You'll feel like you've put in minimal EFFORT — almost as if you didn't trim them at all. How ironic! But save your breath; there are still some final loops to go.

Now, it's time for the ride's full throttle. This duck dog wouldn't be complete without their webbed feet. Apply the finishing touches by trimming the hairs between each toe. My goodness, would yah look at that! Your hairy one's feet are hairy no more.

With a trim here and a trim there, their

original dog feet feature will begin to reappear.

There's one last thing — a surprise loop. These hounds' nails grow slower than other breeds, so this will be a quick, upside-down twirl. A clip here and a clip there, and your Nova grooming quest comes to an end.

But remember, this journey never truly ends — it's a year-round responsibility to keep their care in check. Can we get a Yippie!

What a fun, emotional rollercoaster ride of gundog care with your Nova Scotia Duck Trolling Retriever.

CHAPTER 6

The Beagle Grooming Banquet

Marveling at the thought of cooking? Ahem, I mean "grooming your beagle!" Well, that clever hound of yours will sense something's up. Yep, something's cooking alright. Your mini-muscular Sherlock Holmes, the master of tracking scents, is on high alert!

His howls start echoing the moment he catches a whiff that it's bathtime. With over 220 million scent receptors, that little black nose of his is the best in the business. One sniff of doggy shampoo, and he's bolting for the nearest exit.

Oh my, he's fast! Look at him go — he's faster than you can say "fetch!"

Once you wrangle that rascal, it's time to clean him up. Start with his luxurious, drape-like ears. Keeping them clean is as essential as washing your own hands. Gently lift an ear and use a pup wipe to clear away any surface dirt.

Then, apply a few drops of a tail-wagging-approved ear-cleaning solution to a cotton pad and give those ears a thorough yet gentle cleaning. Eww, gross! But hey, someone's got to do it.

And don't forget to dry them off! Beep, beep, beep — oh, that's just the microwave timer you set. See? All done in a flash.

Next up is shower time! And yes, I mean your

shower, too. Grab your loofah! Beagles are the ultimate crumb-snatchers, and they're bound to get a little dirty from all that scavenging. So, it's bathtime for them, and brace yourself for a splash zone event like no other.

Lather them up with a quality-grade aroma-scented shampoo, and follow up with a generous helping of conditioner. But watch out — these clever little hounds might think it's "dinner time" and try to make a break for it before you can even get them seated and served. Having your own flatware handy — your trusty loofah — might not be such a bad idea after all.

As they shake off that excess bathwater, get ready for a super-soaker showdown. But hey, easy there! Your furry friend just wants to make sure there's room for you at the table — or, in this case, in the bath.

Drying them off with a single towel is just

the appetizer; the main course is yet to come. And you guessed it — it's the HAIR!

Gee whiz, all this grooming feels like preparing a full-course meal!

Beagles are year-round shedders, and the Equigroomer brush can easily double as your steak knife, cutting through and removing all those dead hairs, especially from their undercoat.

Sweeping up their fur and filling a trash bag with it is like finishing off a hearty meal and cleaning it up too. By the end of this grooming session, your beloved Beagle's flag tail will be sticking straight up, a sure sign that he's had enough and is ready for dessert. Because what's a meal without a Scooby snack?

After making it through the entire grooming experience, your hound has definitely earned it — he's cleaned his plate!

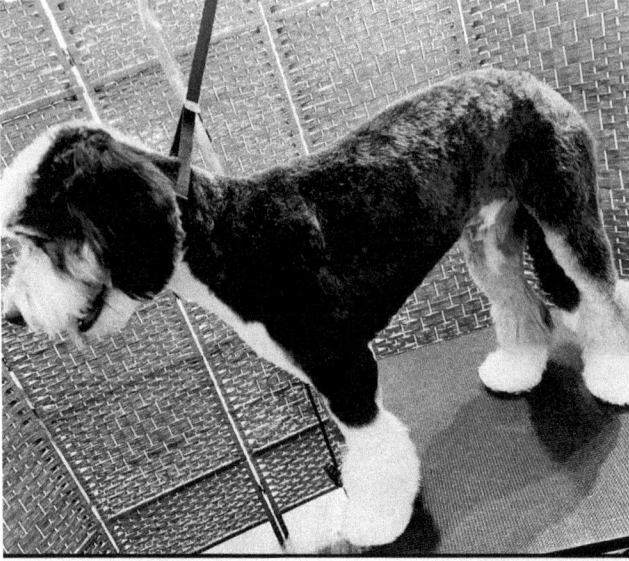

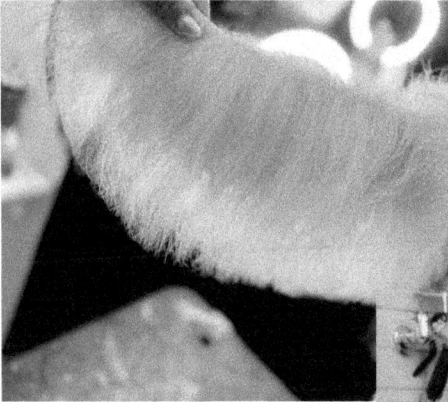

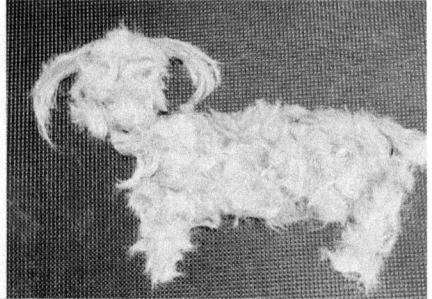

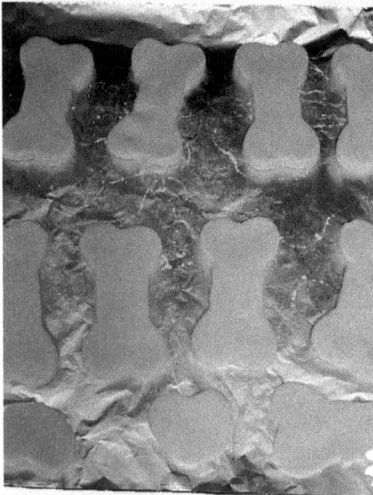

Grooming Fun!

CHAPTER 7

Pom-Pom Pomeranian Spa

Glitz, glamour, and sparkles galore! Welcome to the most exclusive grooming salon in town — your very own living room. Drum-roll, please... Your VIP (Very Important Pup) client today is none other than your precious Pomeranian! The fluffiest, most high-maintenance customer your home spa will ever encounter.

This isn't just a groom — it's an experience,

baby! Your Pom gets to choose their luxury service — no haggling on this package.

'Grr... Yap! Yap! Yap! Yip! Yip! Yip!' Bring out the pom-poms to cheer your vibrant, vivacious, and energetic tyke. And in a whisper voice, 'Good luck!'

You'll start your Pommy's spa day with a slicker brush and deshedding rake, removing enough fur to knit a sweater — a fluffy one at that! With all that shedding, you might even start a new business selling plush and posh sweaters on Etsy. Cha-ching!

Just be ready for a bit of coughing and a few hairballs floating around. 'Harrumph.' Whew — just clearing out the throat.

Can you believe these puffball pups used to weigh up to 30 pounds? But thanks to a little breed mixing over time, they've shrunk down to their adorable size today. Once you dunk your cotton ball of sassy pants into the water, you'll see them transform from puffy wuffy to something resembling a four-legged rat! Yikes! Cue the hands-on-face-scream, 'Ahhh!' what happened to my paw-bestie? Give them a generous lathering with bubbles galore and marvel at the finest soap suds around.

Next up, only the best of the best conditioners for your high-value client. No cutting corners here. After a deep conditioning session with a few well-placed massages, it's time for the grand finale.

Roll out the heated blankets, honey! Wrap your beautiful Pommy in a warm towel before blow-drying them back to their original, quintessential fluffiness. While soft spa music plays in the background, the atmosphere is just right for your Pom-Pom Pomeranian's finishing touches.

Use grooming scissors to trim any uneven hairs around their ears, paws, and tail. Finally, a gentle nail clip with top-of-the-line clippers wraps up this exclusive full-package service. Don't expect a tip from your cheeky, non-paying client. He's not paying! LOL!

You can now flip your sign from 'Open' to 'Closed.' Close up shop for the day, and chill-ax in another room. After all, you are at home.

CHAPTER 8

Genius German Shepherd

Ready to test your grooming smarts? It's time for a pop quiz — German Shepherd style! Grab your grooming tools, and let's see how well you know this four-legged chess master.

Here's your first question: With ears pointed and head tilted, when it's time for their groom, what will they do? Hmm? Still thinking? Here's a hint, your Germy will decide the best answer to this test. Now, back to the question: What will they do?

    A. Play dead

    B. Make a run for it

    C. Just go with it

    D. All of the above

German Shepherds are clever, especially when it comes to grooming. They might eye that warm bathtub full of bubbles with suspicion — it's just their nature to inspect everything first.

But, ding, ding, ding! The answer is... C. Just go with it! That's right, your confident canine will ace the bathing portion with flying colors.

Moving on to the next step, though, might be a bit more challenging — for you, that is. Now, for the drying round: This double-coated wonder will test your endurance. So... how long can you hold up that dryer nozzle?

A. Towel drying will be quicker

B. Your arm and time will

make that determination

C. Skip the drying — your superdog

will shake it off in its own-

rinse cycle spin

D. None of the above

Tick tock, tick tock... What's your answer?

Woohoo! You got it right. The answer is B. Your arm and time will make that call. Maybe your smarts are rubbing off on your security dog because drying your medium-sized furry friend can be one heck of a workout!

On to the brushing round: Grab your grooming brush and undercoat rake. Does that sound familiar? Here's the question: How many pounds of hair will land on your floor after brushing your boo-bear?

A. Lots and lots - hello!

B. Who's weighing that?

C. The real question is: Who's

cleaning it up?

D. Oh please, you're exaggerating!

German Shepherds shed like it's their job, leaving behind massive tumbleweeds that even Einstein would struggle to figure out how they got into every nook and cranny. Soooo... "zip-a-dee-doo-dah, zip-a-dee-ay, my, oh my, what a wonderful day" (shout-out to James Baskett). The correct answer is A. Lots and lots!

For the final round, let's talk nails. Cutting them down is a no-brainer, especially when your testing ground is:

A. Engineered hardwood flooring

B. Luxury vinyl flooring

C. Bamboo flooring

D. All of the above

Oh yeah! Whoop! Whoop! Winner, winner, chicken

dinner! You got it right! The correct answer is D. All of the above.

Why? Because your loyal protector tends to love what you love — flooring included. But here's a tip: Luxury vinyl flooring offers the best scratch resistance when those freshly clipped toenails hit the ground.

Your German Shepherd — the ultimate defender — will pass the grooming test time and time again, no sweat. They're natural problem-solvers and always up for the challenge, looking forward to that celebratory belly rub afterward.

'Mmm hmm,' 'Ruff, ruff.'

And hey, give yourself a wag of the tail for passing this test, too! You sure know your noble nacho. Now, time yourself for the next grooming session and see how much quicker you can ace it.

CHAPTER 9

Frenchin! French Bulldog

With a decadent croissant in one hand and a rubber grooming brush glove on the other, signals its time to begin this French Bulldog grooming session. Your Frenchie-pooh sits before you with all the elegance of a Parisian poodle as if their name were Pierre.

"Oh, Pierre, Pierre, my dear, where art though?"

Begin by gently brushing your popular breed pooch from its oversized head down to its stumpy tail. This will be a walk in the park, thanks to their minimal shedding.

Engage with your miniature mate as you brush because the soothing strokes of the brush's silky bristles might just lull them to a peaceful nap. A little relaxation never hurts anyone, right?

A light mist from a water sprayer will do the trick for wetting them down as you prepare for a good hand wash. Submerging them in the bathtub? Not a great idea — they're more likely to sink! Their bat ears will stick straight up. Warning, warning, warning!

Your little tyke isn't a natural swimmer, thanks to their flat face and dense body. With more folds in their face than a map of the Paris Metro, it's crucial to carefully clean between the wrinkles of their droopy facial skin to remove buildup, dirt, and debris.

Pat each part of their frog-dog body dry with a lightly scented, pup-approved cloth. This step is vital to prevent infections, especially around their adorable face.

Special care and attention will keep your poochie pooh healthy and happy — most of all, no one wants to deprive your beloved bulldog of living its best doggone life.

Finish up with a good anti-fungal cream to keep any bacterial moisture at bay. Ick... bites nails.

To wrap up this custom Frenchie groom service, you might have been under the impression that your French philosopher was a true Frenchman, but surprise! Their origins are actually from England.

Who knew that Mr. Pierre was really a Preston? What a piping hot cup of tea! 'Hip, hip!'

CHAPTER 10

A Husky Blizzard

A winter storm is coming — brace yourself! Your Husky's thick white fur looks as if it's been spun from clouds. "Ooh... ahh... wow — a masterful work of art! Isn't she lovely?"

Before you brave the weather — the grooming process — you'll notice the first wisps of fur floating in the air. Amazing! Look at those flurries glide above.

Can you believe it? The first flurries of the winter storm have arrived. Get your snow coat and bundle up! It's the calm before the storm.

Find your snow rake — also known as your deshedding tool — and hold on tight. This powerful grooming tool will help you dig through inches of snow, AKA fur.

Remember, your Wooly Siberian Husky-baby's double coat is built to survive Arctic conditions, so you'll need to bring out the heavy artillery — the SNOW DRYER! Just kidding! But seriously, get your doggy blow dryer and prepare to blast through the thick coat.

Hold on to something because blowing out their coat will release so much hair that you might feel like you're about to be buried alive.

Doing this before bathtime gets you ahead of

the storm — but not so fast. You're still in it. It's chilling to know that blowing Husky-boyz coat twice a year produces massive amounts of hair shed that can last for weeks.

Who in the world has time to clean all that up? (Finger on nose — "Not me!)

Saturating them with water and shampoo, followed by a thick, rich conditioner, might give you a brief reprieve, but the hair snow will still come down in heavy flurries.

Kerplunk!

Before you know it, you're right back in the belly of the storm. So, hold your horses — er, Husky! Okay, saying it louder, hold your Husky! Repeat the undercoat raking process, and yep, you guessed it — bring out the infamous snow blow dryer to dry their coat once more.

Your Siberian sled dog might show some stubbornness, but hey, it's expected — they prefer their independence and have that "Don't tell me what to do; I can figure out this grooming thing myself" attitude.

Eventually, you'll blow enough coats to outfit a whole team of Huskies ready to pull your bobsled across the finish line. Wee! The furry finale is clipping those claws. Be gentle.

Now, give yourself a pat on the back — you've undeniably made it through the blizzard. And don't forget to clean up the mess!

CHAPTER 11

Touchdown Chow Chow

You'd think scoring a touchdown with your fluffy Chow Chow would be a walk in the park, right? Wrong! You wouldn't wish this on your favorite groomer or even your worst enemy.

Grooming your poofy pup isn't just a game — it's the Super Bowl of dog care. Ready? Huddle up your grooming gear because you're about to face off with what you thought was a big teddy bear, but surprise! You're actually staring down a full-blown grizzly. Hands-on face — now scream! Ahh! What have I gotten myself into?

Fweeeet — fweeeet! Oh, don't mind that. That's just the referee blowing the whistle. Time to protect your ears (and maybe your sanity). The first quarter starts with brushing.

You've got to move quick — your Chow's not wasting any time trying to scramble out of this play. Hustle! Hustle! FLAG ON THE PLAY! For those warm-up nibbles — he's testing your reflexes early.

There are a few plays to run to ace your canine cub's dematting debacle. Alright, team, come in close. Here's the game plan: grab the slicker brush like a pro quarterback. You're going to need it to tackle those mats, fluff, and tangles.

This powerful brush will do some magic. It will contour your teddy — pooh's body, making the dematting process a tad bit easier. Pro tip: Chow Chow fur is no joke. Their rough-smooth coat? Tricky business. Double the coat, double the trouble. The key here? Brush in sections, or you'll be out of the game faster than you can say "hairball."

Woohoo! Clap, clap, clap! You're making progress, baby! Cue the fight song: "We ready, we ready, we ready... for y'all!"

Ready, set, HUT! You're moving down the field, and now it's time for some fancy footwork. Get to those little triangular ears and work your deshedding tool behind them with ninja precision.

Whoop — whap, whoop — whap! All that brushing behind the ears? Might trigger a few chomps. Yup, that's right — bite alert! Your Chow

Chow's back on defense. Arf!

Woah — chill, doggie!

Phweeeeet! Another whistle? Really? Flag on the play — for unsportsmanlike conduct. You're up against a tough contender, but no worries. You're in the home stretch! It's time to rinse, shampoo, and condition that furry linebacker. Watch out, though, because lathering this canine comrade may turn them into an absolute army tank. Reminder: this is offense, not defense!

We've got the ball — whelp, grooming tools! Scrub like you're in overtime, then rinse like your championship title's on the line. You're so close to the end zone now — don't fumble the ball!

TIME OUT! TIME OUT! FLAG ON THE PLAY!

Your fluffy linebacker's pulling some serious foul moves with all these bite attempts. But remember, your guard dog is doing what they do best — protecting themselves, even from shampoo.

Hold tight! We're almost at the goal line. The final obstacle? Nail clipping.

Oh boy, it's the fourth quarter, and your Chow Chow's switching to full-on defense mode — metamorphosing cat-like behaviors. Nail clipping = game-winning kick.

Just when you're thinking of kicking a field goal and calling it a day, you dig deep. We're going for the TOUCHDOWN! Hold their paw gently — like a seasoned pro, ease them into each tender clip, and when that big blue-black tongue finally flops out of their mouth? TOUCHDOWN! You've made it, champ! The crowd (you) goes wild!

Don't forget to hand out the post-puppy treats — your baby-boo bear has earned it.

Chow Chow championship trophies for you and

your snuggly linebacker! Now, let's retire that grooming gear and celebrate.

CHAPTER 12

Basquiat of Grooming the Hair/Hairless Chinese Crested

In the realm of canine aesthetics, few subjects are as challenging—or as amusing— as the hairless Chinese Crested. Your eccentric canine is a masterpiece of nature — one must take their time in sculpting.

Roll up your sleeves, you fine artist — you. It's time to create a work of art! Your unmistakable hairless or "Powderpuff" breed is in for a whirlwind of exquisite grooming bliss.

Get your Picasso hands ready. Grooming your elegant beauty requires ambidexterity as both of your hands are important in this process. Hey — didn't you say you were an artist? No excuses here.

Your regal pooch is delicate, so you must be delicate to the touch when handling it at home — I mean handling it in your in-home pup salon, that is. And what shall you need to craft this tyke? Tools. Lots of tools.

The hair on your Crested's head isn't just hair. It's a graceful, wispy crown. Halt! Your ultra-affectionate lapdog demands your soothing combing caresses. Thou shall not be rough!

Oh, how the fine-tooth comb, along with a silky-like pup-approved detangling spray, delicately untangles their knots, ensuring every strand is in its place.

Aht — aht! Come back, Fifi — come back! See there, you were a little too rough. Gentle, gentle, gentle! Okay, now you've got the hang of it. Orchestra, cue the harps! Glide through with the gentleness of a maestro conducting a symphony.

There — you've got it. See how you work your canvas!

Pfffff — pfffff! Blowing something away? Don't mind that — it's only a hairball. An expected flyaway. Although your African hairless dog (can be just that) or coated one — yes, its origins trace back to the motherland, its occasional tresses of fur can lead to sudden fluff.

Achoo! Did someone sneeze? God bless you.

But for those little Crested-eeez with coats, the deshedding brush works like presto in removing loose strands and keeping the coat looking as smooth as a freshly varnished canvas.

Next, it's time to give them a warm bath— their speckled pink skin is ready to be cleaned. Maintain a calm demeanor to keep them quiet as you lather a hyper-allergenic shampoo. Using a rubber bath brush is key!

Your yay-high 'non-finito' or unfinished work of art, as the Italians say — loves the elastic feel of the brush. A lulling massage — but even more, a guaranteed feather duster! No rubber in sight? No worries, even your bare hands can nimbly work into their coat, ensuring your nobleness remains spotless without irritating their sensitive skin.

Listen to the ensemble. Can't you hear them as they sing? "Moisturize, moisturize, moisturize." Ahh, what a lovely Gregorian chant.

SKRRRT! Focus, focus, focus. The most important thing in grooming your Crested carry-around dog is moisturizing.

The hairless part of the Crested's coat needs attention. Their skin can be prone to dryness, so a light, non-greasy moisturizer will keep it supple and glowing. Give Fifi a pristine shine. Ting! Would ya look at that? Your artwork is coming along — but we're not done.

Stroke with your grooming shears to trim those unruly hairs that refuse to conform. Wherefore art thou scissors — your trimming tool? These are not just scissors. They are fine-tuned instruments of precision that are perfect for snipping away excess and shaping Crested's majestic crest. Oh, what a charm it is to see!

Finally, it's time for the finishing touches. The nail clipper for a perfect finish. Pup-safe nail clippers ensure their talons are trimmed to perfection. And a little nail polish, if you may — Fifi wants it!

One last thing. Your temperature-sensitive tail-wagger needs a little aristocratic swag. A stylish, lightweight dress with a fashionable hairbow and a pop of color does the trick, while a cozy sweater in the winter keeps them warm and incredibly satisfied.

You deserve a round of applause. Your Chinese Crested pooch is now front-cover magazine-worthy. Your enhanced living work of art is a masterpiece. A work of art to be envied all around. Let its regalness shine!

Bravo — bravo! Tour dematting force!

CHAPTER 13

On the Clock Doberman Pinscher

Your big boy (or girl) Doberman Pinscher plays no games. Sure, they may be your family pet, but give them two badges — your buddy bodyguard, aka, your guardian, not only takes their most important job of protecting you seriously, but they also guard something else: themselves from grooming time.

Bow-wow! Your on-the-clock canine custodian is pulling a double duty. But don't worry, the barking will eventually stop — "if" you do it right. Not a groove and smooth but a groom and smooth. Let's do this!

Hold on — don't run off now! Your "Dobey-pooh" won't be working a full eight-hour shift, more like a mini-shift. Thank heaven — this won't take forever. Their smooth, short-haired coat doesn't require any overtime grooming. So, let's get this done!

Focus.

Arm yourself with your rubber mitt brush. Mmm hmm, make sure it's rubber — they like that. Look at them wagging their itty-bitty tail, as calm and happy as can be... for now. Ha! Sike! Show your protector-pooh proof.

Hold up that suspicious red object (the brush) and say, "Attention! Attention! Mr. Dober, this is just a comfy red brush to smooth you out. No harm, no foul. Scout's honor!"

Owners, you've got to socialize your four-legged defender early — both to grooming *and* people! It's a preventative measure straight out of the doggie bylaws book, section 4.107.235-6: introducing your hanging-tongue pup to the idea of dog spa days and society will make grooming your rough-rider rascal easier with minimal restraints or, worse, a fur fight!

Duck!

Place them in a half-full tub of water or wet their sleek coat, and your beautiful black "Pinchy" glistens like a diamond as the light reflects off their muscular body. Add a dime-sized amount of a quality dog shampoo and conditioner combo — it'll enhance your little security man (okay, not so little). Oh, and pick a good scent. After all, a good-smelling pet is a huggable pet.

Who doesn't want a fresh-smelling muscle man?

Next up, no surprises here: those unique ears! Clean them regularly to shave hours off your grooming routine — and keep your vet bills low. You already pay a hefty salary to your bodyguard: quality food, shelter, love — it adds up! Keeping your fearless friend clean saves you from spending extra.

Haven't you learned? Money doesn't grow on trees! Sheesh!

Look at that. You're making strides with this at-home grooming thing! Now, wrap up your speedy German Gonzalez. A warm towel is their tuxedo uniform. Throw in a spiked neck chain — gotta keep up appearances, right? A sleek, no-nonsense, TikTok-on-the-clock companion.

Nothing wrong with a little aesthetics!

We're about 30 minutes in this groove — oops, I mean, groom! Don't forget we're on the clock. Hold up. Wait a minute! Is Mr. Dobey flexing his muscles while you're clipping his nails?

According to section 87.412.93-4 of the doggie bylaws book, this isn't your first rodeo unless your watchdog's still a puppy. Use canine-approved claw clippers and give those nails a nice shape-up.

Clip their claws regularly — biweekly, preferably — so neither of you end up facing an assault charge. You know how you both like to overreact. And... cue laugh. It was a jokey joke... with some truth.

As your shift wraps up, the doorbell rings. Ding-dong! Just like that, your intelligent-breed comrade is back on their night shift, ready to protect and eject any unwanted (or even wanted) guests on your premises.

Because for a well-groomed bodyguard, the job is never done! Bow-wow!

CHAPTER 14

Beauty Bichon Frise

Look up! It's a bird, it's a plane... oh, wait! It's a white, fluffy cloud! Soft, snuggly, and soooo freaking cute — it's your poochie — pooh! Your beauty, the Bichon Frise! She's incoming and ready for a good groom.

Playful as ever, she teeters around when it's spa time. Let's face it, your precious cargo is bursting with excitement for this moment. But gather your courage because grooming her isn't for the faint of heart. Someone pass the accordion fan and flick that thing open and fan yourself — whew... that's right, catch your breath before the jolly games begin.

Only the best of the best for this comfort-loving tyke. Place her in the tub with just a bit of warm water — now's not the time to test her swimming abilities. Sure, she can swim, but you're here to clean, not dive into that adventure! Otherwise, you'll be stuck on step one for eternity.

Told you, she loves to play... and play... and play. Geeze! Does this small, non-sporting dog ever stop? No way it's not a sporting dog — because she's definitely got sport! Well, not that kind of sport. If you know, you know. That one's for kicks and giggles. Hope you laughed. Google it if you must.

For this fluffy wonder, you'll need a top-grade whitening shampoo — yes, the purple kind. Go figure, right? The things that make you say "hmm." But trust me, this premium soapy goodness is key to keeping your snuggle-wuffaloo's coat looking like a marshmallow, bright and fluffy.

Say yes to the fluff! And did you know her fluff is hypoallergenic? Yep, no itchy, watery eyes for you. Don't forget the conditioner — twin essentials! You and your pup can't live without it.

Everyone needs better hair manageability with less frizz, right? Now, nod your head in agreement... riiiiiight!

Like us humans, your prancy Frise-Frise wants a clean, clear face. Who doesn't? (Put your hand down, silly.) So, what's the secret to getting your cheerful, bouncy fur baby's face all cleany-clean?

A tearless stain wipe!

Ding, ding, ding! You're right. And while you're at it, splurge on the double-eye stain protection wipes — doggie-approved and top-tier!

As playtime in the tub comes to an end (I see you caved), the next game is already in motion. Hope you've got your sneakers on because it's time for the cat-and-mouse chase as she dodges the low-warm setting of the blow dryer.

Keep going until she's fully dry. You're in for some fun! "... nine hundred and ninety-seven, nine hundred and ninety-eight, nine hundred and ninety-nine... and one thousand!"

Hallelujah, she's dry! Your little cloud cub is now fluffy and white as if she's floating in the sky. Aww, how cute! Love to see it.

Out of breath yet? Grab that fan and cool off because, as playful as things have been so far, this next part is no joke — curved shears!

One wrong snip and your cute Bichon might look like someone took a bite out of your cream pie. Yikes!

As you sculpt your little lapdog, it's crucial to step back and give her a good look, carefully rounding her head. Paws! Ha ha. I mean, pause! Be sure you're using scissors only to trim their hair. And don't forget the body — trim it with thinning shears for that perfect petite blend.

Keep her looking cute! (I mean, keep her *super* cute!)

Finally, as this playful groom day nears its end, there's one more thing you need to do. What now, you ask? You've guessed it! Round those paws into little cotton-ball bottoms.

Step back again and gaze at your Beauty Bichon Frise's face. She'll be gazing right back at you with those gorgeous round, dark eyes. Check for any stray hairs and round out more where needed.

After all, her face is her moneymaker, right?

All done!

Set your cloud of joy free to roam the clear blue skies — or, more likely, your messy living room full of cloud dust. Because... guess what? She's ready to play again — with you!

CHAPTER 15

Marvelous Mongrel Mixed-Breed Mutt

One dog, two dogs, three dogs, four... with a face only a mother could love (and maybe a few others), mixed breed dogs come from a wild variation of parents. But, hey — aren't we humans a bit like that too? Mixed up, shaken together, and a little stirred with a dash of this and a sprinkle of that?

Ooh wee!

Purebred, shmur-bred. Your marvelous Mongrel is just right — just as cute, just as perfect. Their uniqueness goes a long way! And don't you forget it.

Whether they're tall or short, skinny or chunky, double-coated, straight-haired, or curly, with so many breeds rolled into one, you're just hoping for the best outcome during their groom. But no matter what, you love them to pieces.

Pause for a moment, find your mixy master, and give that rascal a hug, a belly rub, and a spoonful of peanut butter to butter them up for their spa treatment!

If your mixed breed is smooth or has an extra-extra coat, grooming will be much easier. YAY! Can I get a whoop, whoop? Okay, pump the brakes on that premature celebration — because not knowing which breed your furry mutt takes after the most can send you into a panic.

But don't worry! A deshedding shampoo and conditioner combo is your best bet. Toss in some ear wipes to clean their ear canals and a dog-friendly toothpaste to keep those teeth sparkling.

Quick commercial break, and here's a safety message from our sponsors: "Never, ever, EVER use human toothpaste on your Mongrel-bae — or any dog for that matter! Human toothpaste ingredients can be harmful to them, so stick to tail-wagging paste only!" Got it? Good!

Now, back to your regularly scheduled program.

Tricky, tricky! It's getting really tricky! Things are about to get tough — trimming those nails is always a challenge. Umm... actually, that's almost every dog breed. Ha ha! Just be careful.

Now, let's zoom in on their hair texture.

Ruff! Ruff! Aarf! Aarf! Woof! Woof! I did mention they're a mixed breed, right? All barks matter! Whether curly or wavy, you've got decisions to make.

Feeling overwhelmed? Don't be. Just pick the breed they resemble the most and go with it! Don't overthink it, or your head might start spinning. And if you're unsure, you can always ask your local veterinarian. "Hey, Dr. Vet — ID my Marvelous Mongrel, please!"

Whatever you decide they are will guide their cut and style.(Note: pointer finger raised) Multiple breed variants mean ALL hands on deck — A-L-L! Of course, you know how to spell. Break out the full grooming kit: clippers, clip combs, shears, thinning shears, combs, slicker brushes — the whole shebang.

Snip a bit, clip a bit, shave a bit — it's all about bits of many breeds. There you go —

you've got this! Once you achieve the desired look for your dog, there's not much more you can ask for.

Add some finishing touches — a cute bow, a handsome bowtie, or maybe just a simple bandana to polish up your sweet baby's look.

Aww... you're on to something now!

Reassure your crossbreed darling with lots and lots of love — no matter their mix. One thing that doesn't need figuring out is your love for them and theirs for you.

Mwah!

PAW

MYTH-BUSTERS

PAW MYTH-BUSTERS

Paw Truths or Tales

Different is as different does. Even within the same breed, no two dogs are truly alike. There's a little bit of this and a little bit of that, each pup having its own paw print — you know, a paw-paw ID. Chuckle chuckle.

While many dog myths have a pinch of truth, not all of them are necessarily factual. But hey, who's keeping score on whether your dog's mouth is really cleaner than yours *(oh my)* or if dogs can see ghosts?

Paw Truths or Tales, we're busting these myths! Woof — Woof!

PAW MYTH 1

Do all dogs bite?

They have teeth, don't they? Yes, indeed, they do! But most dogs do not bite unless they're scared or provoked. If untrained or possibly a stray, that little darling doo can bite unprovoked.

Ouchy!

So, use caution and give that dog some space—especially if its tail isn't wagging like it's doing the boogie-woogie.

It's always best to approach with care and let the dog initiate contact when it's feeling friendly!

Ruff, ruff! H-U-R-R-O-O-O! (Hello!)

PAW MYTH 2

Do all dogs shed?

Nope! Not all dogs shed. This could be due to their breed or simply a lack of hair. Fewer dog hairs mean less sneezing and less cleaning up after them.

Sounds like a win-win, right?

— Ohhh yeah!

PAW MYTH 3

Are all dogs born with dewclaws?

Sort of — kind of! Most dog breeds come with front dewclaws, while some are born without them or may form them later on in life.

You know, the weightless thumby-thumbs and big toes of the canine world that can help them with their grip. Say — what? Get the grip outta here!

Breeds like the Norwegian Lundehund, St. Bernard, and English Bulldog can have dewclaws on both the front and back legs, and some even have double dewclaws on their hind legs!

Quite the handy feature, right?

Can you teach an old dog new tricks?

Ha! Of course, you can! Just have a bit of patience, especially for those rascals up there in doggy age, as it may take a little bit longer to learn — and that's if they want to.

Dogs are incredibly smart, and like us, their brains can still absorb new info — even if they've been around the block a few times.

With some dedication, you'll have Sparky jumping through the hoops, playing dead, and catching frisbees before you know it.

Just watch out for Jax — he's already fetching like a pro!

PAW MYTH 5

Can dogs eat all human food?

Not exactly! While some human foods can be shared in small amounts, things can get messy later, if you know what I mean.

The best move? Ask your vet first, as some human foods can be harmful or even fatal — for your dog. And yes, that goes for medications, too!

So, think twice before offering Rusty a bite of your spaghetti and meatballs; maybe sing, "On top of spaghetti, all covered with cheese..." instead! (Shout out to Bob McGrath for that catchy tune!)

PAW MYTH 6

Are dogs color-blind?

Well, not so true. While dogs can't see the full spectrum of colors like humans, they aren't stuck in a black-and-white world either.

It's true that dogs cannot see every color. Surprisingly, some dogs can see blues, grays, and yellows — just not the entire rainbow. Yep, red and green look like shades of gray to them.

But don't worry — what they lack in color vision, they more than make up for in their sense of smell, which is up to 100,000 times stronger than ours, according to dog experts.

"Hey, Duke, maybe lay off the sniffing frenzy for a minute!"

PAW MYTH 7

Does my dog love me?

This isn't a myth; your dog absolutely loves you! And they show it in all the sweet, quirky ways: they follow you around, sleep near you, lean against you, and tote your stinky shoes and smelly socks like a prize possession.

They greet you excitedly when you get home and hold eye contact with you like you're the best part of their day — because you are.

All signs show their love for you is everlasting. From wagging tails to warm cuddles, your dog's love is loyal and true.

No myth-busting needed.

Your dog loves you unconditionally!

About the Author

EVELYN GONDER, hailing from the heart of Richmond, Virginia, has a lifelong connection with dogs, which began during her childhood when she spent time with her grandfather, a Doberman Pinscher breeder. Through the years, dogs remained a constant in her life, offering comfort, especially her beloved pitbull, Freeway, who helped her through personal losses. With over two decades of experience as an entrepreneur, Evelyn built a successful pet grooming business. Now, she's channeling her love for dogs and grooming expertise into writing. Her debut book, Paws & All Tales And Tips, not only aims to inspire future groomers but also adds a comedic spin, showcasing humor and joy in dog grooming. This lighthearted approach reflects her deep passion for dogs and her belief in the importance of embracing the fun side of the grooming profession.

Freeway